Dear God, Where Were You?
...In the Details My Child

Christian Yulander Waldon

Dear God, Where Were You?

Trilogy Christian Publishers A Wholly Owned Subsidiary of Trinity Broadcasting Network

2442 Michelle Drive Tustin, CA 92780

Unless otherwise noted, all scripture quotations are taken from the King James Version of the Bible. Public domain.

Photographer for author photo on back cover: Brian Christian. Stylist for author's photo: Lindsay Waldon.

Rights Department, 2442 Michelle Drive, Tustin, CA 92780.

Trilogy Christian Publishing/TBN and colophon are trademarks of Trinity Broadcasting Network.

For information about special discounts for bulk purchases, please contact Trilogy Christian Publishing.

Trilogy Disclaimer: The views and content expressed in this book are those of the author and may not necessarily reflect the views and doctrine of Trilogy Christian Publishing or the Trinity Broadcasting Network.

Manufactured in the United States of America

10 9 8 7 6 5 4 3 2 1

Library of Congress Cataloging-in-Publication Data is available.

ISBN: 978-1-64773-538-8

E-ISBN#: 978-1-64773-539-5

Dedication

There is no other person to whom I can legitimately dedicate this book to other than the Author and Finisher of my faith, Jesus Christ. I'm sure this sounds like a cliché to some, but to others this is a true testimony of God's goodness. Each trial and tribulation in my story encapsulate God's goodness, love, mercy, and grace for me and over me. God had a plan for my life even before my turbulent entrance into this world. God used each intricate detail as a catalyst for His ultimate plan of salvation for my soul. No storm, regardless of its brutality was able to hinder the plan God had for me.

From the depths of my saved soul, I dedicate this book to Jesus Christ.

Acknowledgements

For Lindsay, Kenneth, Kendra, Allen, and my grandson Chase.
Thank you for your respect, trust, and unconditional love!
It's because of you I persist.

To the "Sweet Jesus" preacher, Mother Redden, Holly, and all who
played a role, I say thank you, thank you, and thank you again!

Foreword

This book isn't about Shadrach, Meshach, and Abednego being in the fiery furnace; it's about me and my fiery furnace of abuse, neglect, and rejection. All of which were weapons chosen to destroy and distract me from fulfilling the purpose and plan God had destined for my life. Throughout every trial and tribulation, God's hand consistently and quietly steered me in the direction of his purpose and plan, even when I didn't know he was doing it. The enemy didn't see it coming, and neither did I.

> But as it is written, 'Eye hath not seen, nor ear heard, neither have entered into the heart of man, the things which God hath prepared for them that love him
>
> —1 Corinthians 2:9

I'm sharing my story in hopes of encouraging others and allowing them to see we serve a relevant God who not only cares about every aspect of our lives, but who also is involved.

Regardless of how the circumstances may look, God's plan will prevail.

Table of Contents

Nature vs. Nurture

I remember it like it was yesterday. My eyes were like heavy dark clouds refusing to allow the sun to shine; tears fell as droplets of rain. My past flooded my mind. I muffled the sound of sobs coming from my mouth as I sat on the floor in my bedroom closet; I didn't want my children to hear me crying. I couldn't help but wonder through the sobs—*where had all my strength gone?* If I were nothing, I was a strong Black woman! My life was finally coming together. Why cry now? I didn't have time for tears or anger! Sitting on the closet floor drowning in tears brought back a lifetime of pain and anger—things I thought I had overcome. Pain and rejection were a constant in my life; I took them in with the breeze—thinking every breath I inhaled made me stronger, and I was determined to exude strength. That's all I've ever had.

> The LORD is their strength, and he is the saving strength of his anointed.
>
> —Psalm 28:8

My six-pounds-eleven-ounces body swam through Mommy's birth canal in a sea of amniotic fluid made up of pain and rejection. There were no bright lights as I approached the shore of life; instead, there was a sign that read "Caution, Whirlwind Ahead." My mind went back, and I could see Mommy and I sitting in the dining room at that old hand-me-down round table I had from the time we moved to Marietta. I can't recall who gave us the table, but it was sturdy with orange, yellow, and green stripes overlaid on a white background; the table had four bright orange chairs that swiveled. The leather-like covering on the chairs had a few rips and slits. If the chairs could talk, they would attest to the pain and rejection I bore over the years.

Before I formed thee in the belly, I knew thee; and before thou came forth out of the womb, I sanctified thee...

—Jeremiah 1:5

Mommy had recently been diagnosed with AIDS and had come to live with us in our three-story townhouse in Smyrna. It seemed like only yesterday she found out she was HIV positive and had colon cancer, now AIDS. I wasn't too excited about having Mommy live with us. I must admit I was somewhat afraid of AIDS, but I had no choice; she was my mother and had no other place to go. It was my duty to help her just as I had when she was diagnosed with HIV and colon cancer.

Honor thy father and thy mother, as the LORD thy God hath commanded thee...

—Deuteronomy 5:16

I spoke extensively with infectious disease and oncology doctors, nurses, and other caregivers to learn as much as I could about HIV, AIDS, and how to best protect myself and my children while caring for Mommy. I became a bleach disinfecting and T-cell watching Queen! We had enough room in the three-story townhouse where Mommy had her own room and access to an exclusive bathroom. An exclusive bathroom wouldn't be needed for long because Mommy soon began having to wear diapers that barely clung to her paper-thin skeletal frame. One of the side effects of the antiviral drug cocktail Mommy took was incontinence.

It didn't take long before AIDS started wreaking havoc inside Mommy's body and mind, and there was nothing anyone could do. Mommy used to say she wasn't afraid to die. She just prayed to God that he would not let her get the dark spots and lesions on her face and body, as so many with AIDS did get. God answered her prayers. When Mommy passed away within two months of our conversation on May 20, 1994, the beautiful paper sack colored skin on her face didn't have a mark on it. If it weren't for her sunken eyes that stared mindlessly back at you like two deep black holes, no one would know from the neck down that Mommy had AIDS.

Mommy was always one for speaking her mind and not holding back, which is why it wasn't shocking when she looked at me while we were sitting at the dining room table having one of the last conversations we would ever have and said, "You were an ugly baby when you were born! You were black with a lot of smooth jet-black hair covering your entire head; you looked like a hairy rat!"

Death and life are in the power of the tongue.

—Proverbs 18:21

Mommy went on to tell me she told the nurse to "take away that ugly baby; that is not my baby! I have had two beautiful daughters!" Her words spun in my ears like a whirlwind. Once I gathered myself, I immediately thought about two things. Did Mommy not know her words of death spoken over me that day had latched on to my soul for dear life just as my lips latched on to her nipples for sustenance. I had gone my whole life thinking I was ugly. My other thought was of my sisters and how Mommy was right; my sisters were beautiful babies. They could give the Gerber baby a run for his money any day.

I have my sisters' baby pictures to prove how beautiful they were. Grandma gave me the pictures after her and granddaddy's home flooded during the 2009 floods in Georgia. Ironically, my sisters' pictures were two of the few that didn't get destroyed in the flood. My baby pictures also were not destroyed in the flood because there were none of me to be destroyed. I have never seen any baby pictures of myself anywhere, not even in my own home. Other than me, grandma had baby pictures of all her grandchildren nailed to her walls or sitting on end tables and credenzas.

As Mommy continued talking, I recalled having heard the story about my conception before. Mommy told me years earlier that she and my father were good friends, and one rainy night, he gave her a ride home from the cafe. I can still picture that iconic bright yellow cafe just sitting in the middle of a rural residential neighborhood within walking distance of my grandparents' home. Somehow, Mommy and my father ended up behind Causey Chapel Church; I was conceived that night. For some strange reason, I've always thought there was something special about my being conceived behind a church, and my grandmother having named me "Christian." I guess I needed to believe there was something special about myself. Obviously, Grandma was familiar with Romans 4:17, "...calleth those things which be not as though they were."

Mommy and my father never slept together again because my father was a married man with a family, and their sleeping together had been a mistake. My father did the best he could to include me in his life. He made sure his wife and my half-siblings knew me. I have two older half-sisters and had an older half-brother who is now deceased. The younger two accepted me as their sister, but I believe the oldest half-sister resented and somehow blamed me for what happened. I didn't get the chance to really know and experience my father's love the way my half-siblings did. My father was shot in the head and paralyzed before I was old enough to really know, enjoy, and appreciate him.

This part of the story Mommy was sharing now was new to me. Even though the story was insulting, I listened to Mommy with humility and meekness; I was glad to have Mommy's attention all to myself. As Mommy spoke, I saw what looked like sadness, despair, and remorse in her thin face. I'm not sure if any of those emotions were for me, but something in me hoped they were. Once I refocused, Mommy was saying the nurse said, "If you don't want your baby, I'll take her!" Mommy said it was the nurse's tone and facial expression that jolted her back into reality like a bolt of lightning.

Mommy wasn't one to be outdone and with a fierce tone and stoic facial expression of her own said, "You can't have my baby!"

The memories of this conversation ran through my mind as I continued crying, sitting on my closet floor. I asked myself... *How would my life have been if that nurse had walked out of Kennestone Hospital March 23, 1969, with me in her arms? Why didn't I take advantage of my time with Mommy and tell her how I felt about many things that happened in my life—and was I so ugly that no one cared about me being raped as a little girl?*

When my father and my mother forsake me, then the LORD will take me up.

—Psalms 27:10

"I can't believe they let him get away with raping me!" I said those words out loud repeatedly. This was the first time I had ever given the incident some thought and called it what it was, rape. I stopped sobbing for a moment and decided then and there that I would do something about Bobby having raped me when I was a child. I refused to be discarded like debris left from a tornado. It didn't matter that I was an ugly little girl or that it happened over two decades ago. I deserved justice! I would make Bobby pay for what he had done to me. I threw the jeans I used to muffle the sound of my sobs to the floor, wiped my eyes, took a deep breath, emerged from my closet, sat on my bed, and remembered the rape like it was yesterday.

> Dearly beloved, avenge not yourselves, but rather give place unto wrath: for it is written, Vengeance is mine; I will repay, saith the Lord.
>
> —Romans 12:19

I was outside alone when Bobby asked me to go with him to his apartment. I didn't think anything about it; everyone knew Bobby. He didn't talk a lot; he would just come outside and stare at us kids while we played. Bobby told me to keep quiet as we tiptoed to his apartment. He lived with his mother and brother. We went into a bedroom. I don't remember the details of what happened once we got into the room. I just remember lying on a small bed with him on top of me, and I remember I felt a lot of pain; I don't recall crying. *I am supposed to be a "big" girl and not cry.* Bobby may have said those words to me; I don't know. When he finished, he eased me out of the apartment and told me to go down the backstairs and not to tell anyone.

I did what Bobby told me to do and went outside and started playing with the other kids who had now come outside. *Am I in shock because surely the pain was just as profuse as the blood that soaked my pants?* Somehow, I continued playing with the other kids until Sonya pointed and yelled, "There's something on your pants!" I looked down and saw a sea of red and ran in the house. My aunt Stephanie was sitting in the living room when I ran inside. She jumped up and started screaming for Mommy! Mommy came running. I remember her asking, "What is it?" She took one look at me and said, "Oh my God!" They kept asking me what happened. I didn't say a word. I remembered Bobby told me not to tell anyone. Mommy and my aunt changed my clothes and put me in bed. A few minutes later, Mommy came to check on me and pulled back the covers. The sheets and bed were drenched in my blood.

I remember coming through from the anesthesia and seeing two nurses standing together crying; one of the nurses looked very familiar. I thought they were crying about me; I wanted them to look and see that I was okay. They didn't see that I was awake. When I looked up again, I saw Mommy crying with the nurses. I later found out a very popular pimp by the name of Red had been murdered the night before. Their tears weren't for me after all. Red and my mother were friends; they were from the same small town of Austell. Red and his women lived in the same apartment complex in Atlanta. *At that time, I didn't know the women were "working" women.* I just knew Red lived with four or five Black and White women who were very pretty and always very nice to us; this explains why the nurse looked familiar to me; I had seen her before at Red's apartment.

Once Mommy and the nurses realized I was awake, they ran over to check on me. The nurses fluffed my pillows, changed the padding on the bed, and gave me some medicine. Before they left, they asked if I needed anything and told me they would soon return to check on me. The nurses were very nice. When they left, Mommy told me I almost bled to death, and the doctors had to rush me into surgery because my innocent body had been ripped apart. In a gentle voice, she insisted I tell her who had done this to me. I finally told her it was Bobby. I told her he said for me not to tell anyone. For the first time since the rape, I cried like the little girl I was.

...God shall wipe away all tears from their eyes.

—Revelation 7:17

When I got home from the hospital, everyone treated me special for the first few days. I remember Bobby's mom coming over to our apartment, crying and apologizing. I heard her explain to Mommy that Bobby was "slow" and didn't know what he had done. She pleaded with Mommy not to call the police or press charges. I heard Mommy ask her, "Do you not realize what he did to my baby?" Hearing Mommy say the words "my baby" made me feel special. After that day, I never heard anything else about the rape; it was gone with the wind. Nothing was ever done for me or to Bobby. *I've often wondered; did they forget I was a child, and where were Child Protective Agencies and Mandated Reporters?*

Casting all your care upon him; for he cares for you.

—1 Peter 5:7

After sitting on my bed replaying the rape over in my mind, I'm not quite sure who I called over the phone, but as soon as the woman on the other end of the phone said, "Hello, how may I help you?" the tears started dropping from my eyes yet again. I didn't want to cry, but no matter how hard I tried, I couldn't stop the tears. Between droplets of tears, I told the strange woman on the other end of the phone the entire story about the rape. She listened, never interrupted, and with a gentle voice she apologized for what had happened to me and agreed with me that something should have been done for me and done to Bobby. She said it would be almost impossible for me to do anything about the rape; too much time had passed.

The woman on the other end of the phone encouraged me to continue crying. She ministered to me about God being in control. She reminded me how God had kept me thus far and how he would continue to help me. I don't know who the woman was or where she worked—I don't even know her race, but I know God placed her in the right place at the right time. And I knew she was right that I had to leave it in God's hands. God used her to provide the counseling I should have gotten years ago.

> Fear thou not; for I am with thee be not dismayed; for I am thy God: I will strengthen thee; yea, I will help thee; yea, I will uphold thee with the right hand of my righteousness.
>
> —Isaiah 41:10

Peace in the Midst of the Storm

After my rape, life continued as usual. Mommy was always busy with my sisters or herself; both of my sisters were born with sickle cell disease. Mommy spent a lot of time taking my sisters to hospitals and sickle cell clinics. We spent a great deal of time at Grady and Southwest Community Hospitals and the Sickle Cell Clinic on Cascade Road. Each time we went to one of those places, someone would comment on how beautiful my sisters are. They never said anything about me. There were times when Mommy would send me to the hospital to sit with my sisters, and I remember the looks on some of the caregivers' faces when my sisters would say, "This is my sister." This didn't stop me from going to sit with my sisters or helping Mommy. I would do anything to help my sisters and to try and ease Mommy's burdens in hopes of receiving her love and attention.

One day I engaged in a very desperate attempt to help ease Mommy's burdens. Mommy took us shopping downtown. We went to Bakers Shoe Store for shoes, and once again, I didn't ask for the shoes I really wanted, I pretended to want an inexpensive pair of shoes, and that was fine with Mommy. We got our shoes and left the store. Wouldn't you know it, once we got home, we realized I had two left shoes in my box! Mommy was frustrated with the thought of having to go back downtown and return the shoes. I didn't want her to be frustrated, so I put on the shoes and pranced around in front of her to show her the shoes didn't hurt, and I could wear them and would be fine. My prancing and words must have been very convincing; my big right toe leans in an awkward position to this day.

I continued sacrificing my wellbeing and joy anytime I thought it would relieve Mommy of some stress, whether it was by choosing an inexpensive pair of shoes or an ugly cheap dress I didn't really like or want. I tried doing whatever I could. I never asked for much for my birthday or Christmas. I always made sure my Christmas list didn't contain too much, and when I never got the main thing I asked for, I would just say to Mommy, "It's okay." I never asked to go on school field trips or to participate in fundraisers. If I did get an opportunity to attend a field trip; it was free, and I was never able to take a lunch or have spending money. I couldn't get Mommy to buy my school pictures. I always took the small sample picture off the packet and returned my picture packet back to school.

There were other times when my wellbeing and joy were sacrificed, but not by my doing. Mommy never came to any of my school events; she was always too tired. I was a smart kid, and therefore always asked to participate in something. One time, I was all but certain Mommy would show up. It was the day of Fifth Grade Graduation from Utoy Springs Elementary School; I was chosen to give the speech. This was a big deal for me. Mommy bought the white dress I needed, but she didn't comb my hair. I combed it best I could. Mommy always promised the night before to get up early and do my hair, but she never did, not for picture day or even for this special day.

Surrounded by the excitement in the atmosphere, giggles, and music in the background, I constantly peeped from behind the stage curtains hoping to see Mommy sitting among the parents and other family members who were gathering for this momentous occasion. I never did see Mommy sitting in the audience. My feelings were bruised and battered. I gave the speech and tried as best as I could to enjoy the moment. When my classmates asked about my mother and family, I told them they were on the way. To this day, I get a sense of mixed emotions ranging from nostalgia to sadness whenever I hear "The Greatest Love of All." That was the song they played as we walked out on stage in front of a happy applauding audience full of parents and other family members, all but mine.

They that sow in tears shall reap in joy.

—Psalm 126:5

Mommy was overwhelmed with the financial burden of being a single mother with two sick children, and she wasn't the best with budgeting. On any given day, we could come home from school and there would be no electricity for a day or two, or we would find our belongings out on the street because we had been evicted. I'll always remember the humiliation of walking home from school with friends and seeing what was left of our possessions scattered across the lawn. There are no words to describe this feeling. Through it all, Mommy always found a way to have the electricity turned back on, and she always found a place for us to live.

> Fear not; for thou shalt not be ashamed: neither be thou confounded; for thou shalt not be put to shame: for thou shalt forget the shame of thy youth...
>
> —Isaiah 54:4

One time when we were evicted, Mommy had to split us up. I believe my sister Sabrina stayed with my grandparents or my Aunt Tammy. Sabrina was always a favorite and got to go wherever she wanted to go. My brother stayed with Mommy or went with his father. Mommy had my brother Carey three years after me. My brother was a very cute baby. His skin was paper sack brown like Mommy's; he had the perfect nose and a head full of nice soft hair that struggled to form an afro. Everyone thought he was the cutest baby boy; they adored and fussed over him all the time. They especially fussed over his protruding navel. Mommy used to tape a fifty-cent piece over his navel in hopes of flattening it; this was an old-wives tale that never worked. My sister Teresa and I went to live with one of Mommy's friends who lived in Douglasville. It took us a long time to get to his house in Douglasville. I didn't mind; I was enjoying the drive.

Mommy's friend was a very old thin man who looked like a Black Indian. His cheekbones were high and keen; they looked as if they could cut through metal. The old man used to come over to our apartment about once a week. He never visited too long or said much. Once we arrived at his house, his wife came out and looked us up and down before saying, "Hey." Her voice was drier than the leaves that fall in autumn. She had a very light complexion, and she was older than Mommy, but she was not as old as her husband. There were two girls there who were close to mine and Teresa's age. One girl was very light with long curly hair. The other girl was dark. The light pretty girl with the curly hair was the daughter of the thin old man and the mean lady with the dry voice. The darker girl, I believe, was the old man's granddaughter.

Their home was on a lot of land. I looked around for as far as my eyes could see, and there was nothing but land. It was farmland with a garden, horses, cows, pigs, dogs, and chickens. It had a very unusual smell. I can remember the smells of horse manure, hog slop, fresh eggs just hatched from a chicken, and the smell of fresh pork sausage cooking in the morning. The pungent smells blended and wafted through the air. I can also remember how hot the sun felt on my skin. I'd never felt a sun so hot. I was thankful for the scattered pine and oak trees that stood upright beckoning with their branches; they were the only refuge from the hot sun. The beckoning trees, smells, and scenery on the farm provided a false sense of temperate ground.

As time went on, Teresa and I began to adjust to life on the farm as best we could. The mean lady with the dry voice treated us okay, but we knew she didn't want us there. She made sure we knew her daughter and granddaughter came before us, and nothing or anyone came before her daughter. The girls didn't have to play with us or share their toys if they didn't want. But, oddly enough, the girls were nice. When the mean lady cooked, she made sure her daughter was the first to get a plate of food. Although it was the bare minimum, the mean lady did feed and take care of us.

But my God shall supply all your need according to his riches in glory by Christ Jesus.

—Philippians 4:19

Mommy called from time to time to check on us. Teresa always told her she was ready for her to come get us. In my quest not to burden and stress Mommy, I never complained. I always said I was fine, but this wasn't the truth. I desperately wanted Mommy to come get us. I wanted to live wherever she was living. The lady did not like me; she was very mean to me. When she spoke to me, it was with a harsh tone. My plate was made last, and I was always ignored. She was a little nicer to Teresa; I think it was because Teresa was pretty and was ill with sickle cell. After about three months of living on the farm with the thin old man and the mean lady, Mommy came and got us.

I learned to cope with life on the farm just as I had learned to cope with previous situations in my life. I discovered there is peace and comfort in being alone and observing nature.

God, even the Father of our Lord Jesus Christ, the Father of mercies, and the God of all comfort; Who comforted us in all our tribulation...

—2 Corinthians 1:3-4

When Mommy picked us up from the farm, we went to an apartment off Martin Luther King Jr. Drive. We didn't stay there long before moving into a house off Mango Circle. By this time, my sisters were coping with their disease a little better; their sickle cell crisis weren't coming as often, and they were able to spend more time in school. Sabrina and Teresa were already in high school, and I was finishing my last few months of seventh grade at John Carey. My brother was living with his father. Sabrina was attending school on a regular basis, but she was unable to walk with her graduating class; she was very ill during her graduation ceremony.

We lived in a nice home on Mango Circle. Our stepfather had a good job working at the Atlanta Journal and Constitution (AJC). Sabrina was dating a guy she really liked; they made a very cute couple. Teresa was also dating, and they really liked each other. It was very sad when her boyfriend was murdered downtown at Five Points while heading home from having visited with her. Teresa took his death extremely hard. Mommy was still sewing her wild oats; she spent a great deal of her time at a little juke joint about five minutes away from the house.

I was still left to myself. I was not old enough to date, but young men seemed to take an interest in me. I soon found out it was because my body had blossomed. I was referred to as "fine, but not pretty." My being "fine" must have been what caused Robert to set his eyes on me. He was a twenty-year-old young man who lived about four houses down on the opposite side of the street. I never paid him much attention. He would always say little things to me whenever he would see me walking or sitting alone outside my house. At some point, Robert began having sex with me. He would tell me what time to leave school; I skipped classes, and he would be there waiting to pick me up. I was thirteen and in high school. Robert had sex with me whenever and wherever he could. He had sex with me behind my house, in a car, and in his grandparents' home; it didn't matter to him. He never called me his girlfriend or acknowledged me in public; he said it was our secret. I didn't care. In my naïve mind, I thought he liked me; I was glad to have someone paying me some attention.

One day I came to my senses. Robert told me his friend Carter would pick me up from school and bring me to his house. Carter picked me up from school, and we were heading towards the house when Carter suddenly made a left turn down a gravel road. I asked him, "Where are we going?" He said he was making a stop. I could sense a storm brewing, and I started to feel nervous. There were no stops to be made on that gravel road. About half a mile off the gravel road, Carter stopped the truck and reached for me. I slapped his hand and asked him what he was doing. He kept grabbing and touching me. Each time he would reach for me, I would slap his hand away and try to open the truck door. He quickly grabbed the door handle of the truck and pulled the door shut.

We went on like this for what seemed like hours. He finally looked at me and said Robert said it was okay. I told him I didn't care what Robert said. We tussled some more. I remember being so exhausted that I wanted to give in, but something on the inside kept pushing me to resist. Carter finally gave up and took me home. In my heart, I knew he spoke the truth about saying Robert told him it would be okay for him to have sex with me. I never said anything to Robert. From that day forward, I never let Robert have sex with me again.

Though I walk in the midst of trouble, thou wilt revive me: thou shalt stretch forth thine hand against the wrath of mine enemies, and thy right hand shall save me.

—Psalm 138:7

Not long after the incident with Carter, I was sitting in homeroom when I became sick. I went to the bathroom and threw up. It was the oatmeal I had eaten for breakfast. I decided to leave school and go home. Our home was now at Mrs. Jones' house. When I got there, I went straight up to the attic where we were sleeping and laid on the bed. We no longer lived in a nice house on Mango Circle. We moved before they evicted us. Again, we had to split up. Teresa and I were living with Mrs. Jones; she was a friend and co-worker of my grandmother's. She had older children, and they were nice enough to us. We didn't stay with Ms. Jones for too long. Mommy and my stepfather found us another place to live.

We were living in a new place about three months when I started to feel and see my body changing. I think I knew I was pregnant, but I wasn't sure. One day Mommy looked at me and asked me if I was pregnant while at the same time saying, "This girl is pregnant!" *Looks like I didn't stop letting Robert have sex with me soon enough.* I'll never forget the look of despair, pity, and hurt on Mommy's face when she realized I was pregnant. She asked me who was the father. I was too afraid to tell her it was Robert. I kept thinking I would be in trouble for letting this grown man have sex with me. For a moment, I thought about lying and saying it was the teenager who lived next door, but I knew that wasn't the right thing to do. I told her it was Robert. She didn't personally know Robert, but Mommy had seen him, knew of him, and his family.

Whatever Mommy said after that, I don't remember. I was too busy thinking about a baby being inside of me. This may have been the first time I wasn't concerned about pleasing Mommy. I just remember telling her it didn't matter who the father is; I was going to keep my baby. Mommy didn't say a word; she just stared right through me. The impact of being thirteen and pregnant hadn't fully crossed my mind. I was just elated with the thought of finally having someone to love me!

I have loved you, saith the LORD...

—Malachi 1:2

Mommy made me an appointment with an obstetrician. His practice was off Gresham Road in Decatur. He was black, tall, heavy, and looked very intimidating. The doctor never said much to me. Mommy went with me for the first two or three visits; after that, I had to catch the bus and go on my own. As the months passed, catching the bus was a feat within itself; I was huge, and I didn't like going for my prenatal visits. I always felt so ashamed and out of place. I was the only teenager in a waiting room of pregnant adult women. No one was ever rude or nasty to me, but they did stare. *I can only imagine what they were thinking.*

Mommy and I talked a lot during my pregnancy. My stepfather didn't say too much, nor did my siblings. I don't remember my grandparent's reaction to the news of my pregnancy, but I'm sure everyone felt shame and pity for me. They knew being a young single mother was a set up for a perfect storm. My grandmother knew I craved apple pie during my pregnancy; she would often make sure I had it and macaroni and cheese. Mommy continued acting like a barometer; she told me what to expect. She said my life would change because having a baby was "real-life stuff." She told me childbirth would be painful. I responded to her and said, "I bet you I won't cry." I listened to everything Mommy said, but I couldn't imagine my life being any harder than it was. *I was very wrong.*

My water broke, and off to Southwest Community Hospital we went. Once we got to the hospital, the nurse called my doctor; birth was on the horizon. I wasn't afraid to give birth. I just wanted them to stop checking to see how much I had dilated. I didn't like them all in my personal business. I told the nurses I didn't want an epidural; I wanted to naturally experience childbirth. However, once the sharp contractions started, I changed my mind; the pain of childbirth was almost unbearable, but It was too late for the epidural. The tall, heavy, intimidating doctor was there and ready to deliver my baby. With two pushes, Lindsay eased through my birth canal; she was greeted with bright lights of joy and unconditional love. Holding my baby in my arms for the first time felt like a perfect spring day.

While giving birth, I didn't cry. I just prayed the same three prayers I had been praying from the moment I knew I was having a baby. My prayers to a God I didn't know were: "Lord, please don't let me have my baby at thirteen. My due date was within a couple of weeks of my fourteenth birthday, and in my mind having a baby at fourteen would be much better than having one at thirteen. My second prayer was, "God, please let my baby girl be pretty." I didn't want my baby to be ugly. And my last prayer, "God, please let my baby love me!" I knew if God answered these three prayers, my baby and I would make it. When they placed my baby in my arms, I didn't look for ten fingers and toes; I looked to see if she was pretty.

God answered each of my prayers. I had Lindsay one week after my fourteenth birthday. Our birthdays are a week apart on the same day of the week. Lindsay was a beautiful paper sack brown; she looked like her father's side of the family. She was born with an old gentle soul; it showed through her dark piercing eyes. Lastly, my baby loved me unconditionally then and now. We have a mother and daughter bond that can only be explained by God answering my prayers. I didn't really know who this God was, but I knew he answered prayers.

And it shall come to pass, that before they call, I will answer; and while they are yet speaking, I will hear.

—Isaiah 65:24

When word about Lindsay's birth got back to Robert and his fiancée. Robert tried denying Lindsay was his child. He made up stories about hearing I had slept with other men, and his fiancée tried to run me down with her car. I didn't care that Robert didn't want to claim Lindsay; I had enough love in my heart for her, and we would be alright. I couldn't understand his fiancée being angry with me. I was a thirteen-year-old girl when Robert started having sex with me.

At the time, I didn't realize I was a victim of statutory rape. Robert was a grown man who knew better.

Mommy wasn't having any of this mess. She got word to both Robert and his fiancée. The harassment ceased. She made Robert bring money and items for the baby. He did come to the house to see Lindsay and he brought money, pampers, milk, and clothes for her. He did this only a few times. Once Robert saw Lindsay, the denial stopped; she looks just like him. I remember Robert's grandparents wanted to see my baby. I took Lindsay to their home, and they instantly knew she was part of their family. His grandmother fussed at him all the time for not spending time with his child; she wanted Lindsay to know the paternal side of her family.

On occasion, I would let Lindsay spend the night with Robert's grandmother. I allowed her to take Lindsay to Lagrange, Georgia, to meet some more of her relatives. I never knew much about Robert's mother. He lived with his grandparents. This interaction with that side of the family didn't last long. Robert's wife was angry and mean. She was determined to make sure Robert stayed out of Lindsay's life, and Robert was determined to let her. Eventually, I took him to court in order to get some financial support; he fought it every step of the way, but I prevailed. Robert was forcefully supporting Lindsay financially, but I could not force him to spend time with her. This broke my heart for Lindsay; I knew it hurt her to know her father didn't want to have a relationship with her.

A father of the fatherless...

—Psalm 68:5

Forecast: Gloomy

Loving and wanting the best for my baby took precedent over everything in my life. I knew in my heart I would be a good mother to my child. Mommy and my stepfather helped me a lot with the baby; they loved and adored Lindsay. I'll always remember my baby wore real diamond earrings at four months old. We were supposed to wait until she turned six months, but Mommy couldn't wait. I never tried going back to school. Mommy talked about me getting a GED. I wasn't quite sure what that was, but at the time, I didn't care. I needed to find a job, and I did. I had to lie about my age. The jobs I found didn't last very long because Mommy got tired of babysitting, and she and I were beginning to clash like a couple of dust devils.

It seemed as if I never had a moment to myself. Whenever I came home from school or work, Mommy would make me cook and or clean. I felt like Mommy was punishing me because I had a baby. None of my siblings had to do what I did. I remember asking Mommy why this was, and she said, "They don't have children; you do, and you will need to know how to keep a clean house and put a meal on the table."

That they may teach the young women...

—Titus 2:4

Regardless of the adult turn my life had taken, there was still a yearning in me to be a normal teenager. One day during the summer after running errands for Mommy, I went by the neighborhood arcade before going home. I loved playing Pac-Man and Centipede; it was a nice release for me. I didn't have any friends. Parents didn't want their daughters hanging around me, and we never lived any place long enough for me to make any true friends. I knew Mommy would fuss at me for being late. I didn't care; I wanted to play a few videogames and have a free moment.

While at the arcade, some guy I had seen there several times before approached me and offered me a ride home. I knew the owners of the arcade knew the guy. He always laughed and talked with them when he came to the arcade. I still asked the owners if they thought it would be okay for me to get a ride home. They said it would be fine. I was grateful for the ride because I was already late and waiting to catch the bus would make me even later. The guy took me to my house and asked if he could have my phone number. I didn't give him my number. I had no interest in him and couldn't believe he was interested in me. He was handsome and light-skinned. *What did he want with me?*

I got out of his car and went inside the house to get my baby and hear the wrath of Mommy. As soon as I walked into the house she asked, "Who was that?" I told her his name was Keith, and she immediately started talking about I better not bring another baby in her house, and I'm no longer a child, so if I'm going to talk to someone, it better be someone who can help take care of Lindsay. I told her the guy was only giving me a ride home from the arcade, and I didn't like him; he was too old. I regretted having said that the moment the words came out of my mouth. She said, "I'm not running a babysitting service! Get your butt home on time, and if you want to go to the arcade, take your baby with you!"

When I did get a chance to go back to the arcade and Keith was there, he gave me a ride home from time to time. I'm not exactly sure when it happened, but I looked up and Keith was claiming me as his girlfriend. I hadn't had sex with him or anything; he just gave me rides home from the arcade. I remember his meeting Mommy, and her main concern was if he was willing to help me take care of Lindsay. He reassured her he would love and take care of Lindsay like she was his own child. He was true to his word; he started supporting my baby and giving Mommy money. Mommy was happy for Lindsay and me; she saw Keith as a blessing. She never asked me how I felt, and there was no need for me to tell her Keith creeped me out, and I didn't want to be with any man.

> Only be thou strong and very courageous...
>
> —Joshua 1:7

Keith started picking up Lindsay and me and taking us out to dinner, the drive-in and on drives. One evening after having gone to a drive-in movie, Keith and I were sitting in his car for about twenty minutes listening to music; Midnight Star was playing. Mommy stood in the doorway and called my name, "Christie!" I looked at Keith, said bye, and attempted to get out of the car when Keith grabbed my arm and twisted it behind my back. "You better not get out of this car!" I immediately felt urine run down my legs. Tears welled up and burned in my eyes due to the pain from his twisting my arm. I was shocked and confused. I didn't understand what was happening. I knew Mommy wouldn't call my name much longer before coming out to get me, and this man was hurting me while telling me I better not move. He finally let go of my arm and said, "From now on, you do what I tell you to do." That was the first time Keith put his hands on me, but it certainly would not be the last.

> Many are the afflictions of the righteous: but the LORD delivers him out of them all.
>
> —Psalm 34:19

Keith continued hurting me. I was afraid and didn't know what to do. Which is why I was shaken the day Mommy said, "Christie, you need to figure out what you're going to do, we have to move." Once again, we were about to be evicted. My mind was racing. I couldn't believe my ears; I knew what Mommy was thinking. I couldn't go live with Keith. I hated him and was afraid he would kill me. I felt sick and ran to the bathroom, where I threw up. I hadn't told anyone about the abuse because I believed Keith when he said I would never be able to get away from him. I know Mommy thought he was a good man and would take good care of me and Lindsay.

The Lord bless thee and keep thee.

—Numbers 6:24

I refused to go with Keith. I got a hotel room on Fulton Industrial. It was during this time living in the hotel when I found out I was pregnant. I was devastated. I didn't want to be fifteen with two children. I used to beg Keith to use protection when we had sex, but he just beat me and did what he wanted to do to me. I knew he wanted me to have his child; he knew it would give him more control over my life. I eventually had no choice but to move into Keith's parents' home with him. I was rarely allowed to see my family. My family still didn't know about the abuse. I believed my sister Sabrina was beginning to suspect something was wrong.

I tried to find some release from Keith by getting a job. Keith's mother kept Lindsay for me while I worked. I worked at Mrs. Winners for about two months during my pregnancy. Keith arrived at my job very early every evening I worked. He sat in the dining room of the restaurant and watched my every move. The managers told Keith he had to wait outside the restaurant because only employees could be in the restaurant during closing. Before I could get out the door, Keith would start fussing and accusing me of being too friendly with the male customers who came through the drive-thru window. I never tried to defend myself; I kept quiet. Keith told me he was going to make me pay once I delivered the baby. I knew he would, and his words hung over me like a bank of ominous clouds. Mrs. Winners fired me. I know they did it because of Keith. I was disappointed; I would have worked up to my delivery day in order to get away from Keith for a few hours.

After I lost my job, I sat around the house all day with Keith's mother while he worked. He didn't want me to leave the house without him. I could take Lindsay outside in the back, and I could, on occasion, go visit with one of his neighbors. She wasn't good company because she was much older than I. It wasn't until he got home, whenever he felt like coming home, and I answered all his questions about what I had done all day, did we go out and run errands. Those errands consisted of going to *Winn Dixie* and the *Package Store*. It felt like I was locked in a prison.

It didn't take long for Keith to get back to his routine of beating on me. Two days after I came home from the hospital with my beautiful baby boy, Keith beat me. He got angry because I was on the phone. He said I was ignoring him. He jumped up and asked who was on the phone. Before I could answer, he hit me in my mouth so hard that he knocked one of my front eye teeth out of my mouth. I was in disbelief. My very first thought was that I was really going to be ugly now! Uncontrollable tears fell from my eyes as I screamed and yelled, "Why did you do this?"

I immediately picked up my tooth and ran into the bathroom. I rinsed my tooth and put it back in my mouth. A few minutes later, Keith's sister walked in and asked what happened. She saw her mother stomping and fussing at Keith—Keith's mother is deaf. I told her what Keith had done. She cussed Keith out and told him he should be ashamed of how he treated me. She reminded him of how he treated me like a prisoner when I was pregnant with Kenneth. Now, he had the nerve to want to beat me because I was on the phone. Keith said some choice words to her, and they went back and forth until he just grabbed his car keys and stormed out the door. His sister tried to console me, but I couldn't stop crying and thinking about my babies. I was glad Lindsay hadn't witnessed this; she was asleep in the room with Keith's mom, and Kenneth was asleep on the bed in our room.

His sister stopped trying to console me and started yelling and screaming, "You need to leave him!" I wanted her to shut up. I knew I needed to leave Keith, but where would I go. I had two babies; my

CHRISTIAN WALDON

baby boy wasn't even a week old, and he had jaundice and needed treatments. Didn't she know I was tired of being beat? I didn't know what I was going to do, but I was going to do something as soon as I figured out what to do about my mouth.

The very next day, I got Teresa's Medicaid card and went to the dentist. The card was more like a letter than a card. It was a deep amber-colored sheet that had the Medicaid recipient's name, age, and other information typed on it. Back then, no one asked for ID. The dental office was located on the corner of Jackson Parkway and Bankhead. When the dentist examined my mouth, she kept asking me if my tooth had come out completely. I told her, "No, it was just very loose." I believe she knew I wasn't honest about what really happened to my tooth. I don't know how she did it, but she performed a root canal and saved my tooth. I was happy about this but sad about having to go back to the house with Keith. I needed a plan.

A couple of weeks after I got the root canal, I thought I was about to die. Keith came into the bedroom and shut the door. He sat on the edge of the bed. He looked like he had been crying or smoked a joint. I was just sitting there filing my nails; I didn't pay him too much attention at all. I didn't have much to say to him from that day he knocked out my tooth. His mother had the kids in the room with her. Out of nowhere, he jumped up and snatched me off the bed. He pushed me into the corner and started choking me. He was yelling something about killing me just as Corliss's boyfriend had killed her. I didn't know what he was talking about, but I felt myself beginning to pass out, so I stomped my feet and beat on the wall with what strength I could gather.

His mother must have felt the vibrations from my hitting and stomping on the wall and floor; she came and started beating on the bedroom door. This got his attention; he finally took his hands from around my neck and said, "Shut up with your ugly self and wipe your face and if you ever try to leave me, I will kill you!" He opened the

34

door and breezed pass his mother as if nothing had happened. His mother saw my face and knew something had happened. She stomped her feet and fussed at Keith in her own way before he opened and slammed the front door shut behind him.

I was not in safety, neither had I rest, neither was I quiet; yet trouble came.

—Job 3:26

I didn't have time to "plan" an escape; it was time to go. I called Mommy. She and my stepfather had gotten another place to live. It was in Atlanta over by the Braves Stadium. I called to see if I could come home. I told her all the things Keith had done to me. I told her he had threatened to kill me if I ever tried to leave him. Mommy told me to wait for Keith to go to work the next day, and for the babies and me to come home. She told me which bus to catch to get to the house. I memorized everything and did just that. I got myself and my babies out of there while I could.

I would hasten my escape from the windy storm and tempest...

—Psalm 55:8

I later found out what Keith said about Corliss was true. Keith went to high school with both Corliss and her boyfriend. He knew them well. Corliss and her boyfriend had been together since high school. It was said, Corliss wanted out of the relationship, and her boyfriend didn't, so he killed her in the house with her family there.

The next morning when Keith went to work, I started packing our things. I packed everything I thought I would need and could carry on a bus with two babies. I sat and patiently waited for Keith to call me from work; he usually called on his first break. Once I knew he was at work, I got my babies dressed and headed for the door. His mother watched me the entire time. I could tell she was rooting for me, and this would be bitter-sweet for her. She loved those babies. They brought her joy, the joy she had not expressed since her husband passed away. She hugged and kissed the babies, put some money in my hand, and waved goodbye.

I sat on that bus taking in the fresh air of freedom while at the same time feeling uncertain about what would become of mine and my babies' lives. I was fifteen with two babies, no education—not even a GED, no money, or a job. I thought about all the pain my young mind and body had already experienced. I wondered if it would ever get better. Mommy was right when she said my life would change; I never expected this. I found myself in a state of gratitude and grief. I snapped out of my deep thinking and remembered there was a bright spot, Mommy said I could come home, and that's where I was heading with my babies.

For surely there is an end; and thine expectation shall not be cut off.

—Proverbs 23:18

Mommy was happy to see us. Once I got our things settled in our room, she and I talked. She said I should have said something before now. She told me I had to stay away from that "crazy jealous fool!" I knew she was right. I didn't want to see him anyway. My focus was on taking care of my babies. I got a job working at the Mall West End. I worked in an ice cream shop. I rode the bus to and from work. Mommy watched my babies. I enjoyed and took pride in my job. I made sure I was there on time, and I gave it all my effort. I didn't earn a lot of money, but I was happy I was able to help provide something for my babies.

Being back under Mommy's roof had its good and bad days. Mommy was smoking crack on a regular basis, and my stepfather was working a different job; he lost his job of over twenty-something years at the AJC due to his being an alcoholic. Even though nothing had happened to my babies, and Mommy took good care of them, I knew it wasn't safe. Mommy wouldn't be able to watch my babies much longer. I didn't know what I was going to do. I didn't earn enough money for childcare. I thought about possibly asking Keith's mother to help me, but I knew this would be dangerous. I stopped working over the weekends and evenings and started working early on weekdays. Mommy didn't start getting high until later in the evenings.

In the meantime, Keith kept calling and apologizing. I didn't want to talk to him. I was so glad to be away from him. It felt good not always being nervous and on edge waiting for the next round of punches, hits, slaps, or chokes to come. Slowly, I again started noticing the rainbows after a good rain, looked up at the trees, watched the birds, and literally smelled the flowers. I had forgotten how much I enjoyed doing these things. Regardless of how often I ignored his calls and told him no, Keith insisted he had a right to come see his babies. I was able to hold him off for a few months before asking Mommy about it; she reluctantly agreed to allow Keith to come to visit the babies. He apologized to Mommy and me and made up some excuse about not knowing what came over him. He claimed he had never done anything like this to any other woman he dated.

When Keith came to visit, Kenneth was about four months old and Lindsay was about sixteen months . We did a lot of things with the babies. We took them to the park and hung out as a family. Keith sometimes complained about not being able to be with his family every day. He asked if we could spend a weekend at a hotel. I told him

I would think about it. He continued to visit and was nice enough, so I agreed to start going to a hotel on weekends. Thus far, everything was going fine. Keith brought us home and sat with us for a while before catching the bus to go to his house. When he got home, he called and continuously talked about wanting to be back with his family under the same roof. This sounded very promising because I knew my time living with Mommy was short-lived. I also knew Keith hadn't changed.

One day Keith and I were sitting in my room. My room was in the back of the house. The room looked as if someone converted a storage room or garage into a bedroom. The room sat right on the edge of the woods in the back of the house. This evening, it was getting late, and I was hinting at it being time for Keith to leave. He asked me if I was in a hurry for him to leave. Before I could answer, He started accusing me of seeing someone else and wanted to know why I wouldn't ask my mother if he could stay the night. I tried telling him she wouldn't allow it. Keith punched me so hard in my chest; he knocked the wind out of me.

When I caught a short chance to breathe, I started yelling. Keith pushed me onto the bed, grabbed his jacket, and headed for the door. By now, my family was walking towards my bedroom to see what was happening. I was crying and gasping for air while pointing in Keith's direction. Keith was running towards the front door; the bedroom had a clear view from the back of the house to the front door. My family ran behind him, throwing things at his back, and cussing him out. Mommy had one of her friends at the house, and she too joined in cussing and throwing things at Keith as he ran from the house.

And the way of peace have they not known...

—Romans 3:17

After this, we didn't see Keith for a long time. I continued to work and take care of my kids as best I could. Every evening there were several people in the house getting high with Mommy while I was in the back room with my babies. My stepfather came home from his job and passed out drunk; he knew what Mommy was doing, but he was too drunk to care or put a stop to it. And regardless of what I said to Mommy, it always came back to, "You are living in my house. If you don't like what I'm doing, then leave." It didn't take much longer for me to do just that, take my babies and leave her house. It was around one o'clock in the morning when I heard footsteps outside my bedroom in the back of the house. I got up and went into the living room to see what was going on. My stepfather was asleep, and Mommy was sitting in the kitchen in the dark. I told her I heard someone walking in the back of the house. She said she knew and told me to get quiet. She went and woke my stepfather. She told him she owed the drug dealer some money, and the drug dealer said if she didn't pay him, he would come to shoot up the house, and she believed it was him we heard in the back of the house. We sat quietly and helplessly in the dark as if we were waiting for a storm to pass. By the grace of God, nothing happened.

> Thou shalt not be afraid for the terror by night; nor for the arrow that flieth by day.
>
> —Psalms 91:5

When the sun came up, my stepfather had Mommy call the drug dealer. Once the drug dealer arrived, my stepfather paid him and told him not to give my mother any more drugs if she didn't have the money to pay for them. He also pointed in my direction where I was sitting with my babies and said to the dealer, "Man, there are babies in this house." This was the first time I ever heard my stepfather acknowledge or say anything about Mommy using drugs. I was glad he had done this, but it was too late of a move for me. I knew what I had to do. I would deal with the abuse before I allowed something to happen to my babies. Keith never touched my babies.

And all thy children shall be taught of the LORD; and great shall
be the peace of thy children.

Isaiah 54:13

The next day I went to my job and told the owner I had to quit. I
asked if he would go ahead and pay me because I couldn't wait until
payday. He paid me in cash as he always did. He said he was sorry to
see me leave, and if I ever needed to come back I could. I left that job
and went back to Mommy's house and called Keith. He came and
got us and took us home with him. He fussed and talked about how
horrible a mother I had. I didn't say a word, but I thought to myself...
Does he think he's any better?

Fall Foliage

Keith kept his word and got us an apartment, but before this, we moved back in with his mother, where the beatings continued. My sister Sabrina lived nearby his mother's house. Keith and I would sometimes get the babies and visit Sabrina. One day while visiting Sabrina, her cousins stopped by. One of them asked for a glass of water, and I got up to get the water. Sabrina was talking or doing something, so I just offered to get the glass of water. A few minutes later, Keith said it was time to go. Sabrina kept the babies overnight, and I was grateful and excited to have a break. I was ready to leave. As soon as we reached the top of the stairs outside, Keith kicked me down the iron staircase. When he got to the bottom of the staircase where I lay, he said, "Why the heck did you have to get him a glass of water? You must like him." I got up crying with a busted lip, scratches on my arm, and hoping my sister hadn't witnessed this.

Soon after this incident, we moved into an apartment in Mableton. I became numb to the beatings and tried to avoid his triggers, which were many. Keith became violent when he drank vodka, when we were around people, and he thought I was checking someone out, or if he thought they were checking me out. He became violent whenever I spoke of my family. I had to keep my eyes straight ahead when I rode in the car with him. I couldn't close the bathroom door. I couldn't go shopping by myself, and I dare not be too friendly to any man. I soon found out the hard way; there were no specific triggers; Keith was an abuser.

The LORD also will be a refuge for the oppressed, a refuge in times of trouble.

—Psalm 9:9

My mother hated him, and he didn't like her which is why I knew it was going to be a battle when I had to ask him if my mother and

43

stepfather could move in with us for a few weeks. It took me a few days to plan out how I would ask him. I made sure the mood and timing were perfect. With all of this, I still doubted he would allow it. To my surprise, Keith said yes. Mommy and my stepfather eventually moved out of the house over by the Braves Stadium and moved into an apartment. Mommy was trying to do a little better. They let my sister Teresa live with them. Teresa was smoking crack and running the streets. Mommy told me my sister stole the rent money from my stepfather when he passed out drunk; therefore, they needed to move in with us.

In the beginning when Mommy and my stepfather moved in with us things were going smoothly. I walked on eggshells every day, but things were pretty good. One day I came home from work and saw Keith in the kitchen smoking crack with my mother. I couldn't believe my eyes! I looked at him and asked, "What are you doing?" I thought he was going to hit me, but I didn't care. Instead, he walked over to me with bulging eyes and quivering lips, trying to explain he just wanted to try it. I gave my mother a look of disgust. Within a few minutes, he was begging me to give him some money. I refused and went to check on my kids, who were asleep. I took a bath and got into bed. I didn't get much sleep because Keith constantly came in the bedroom begging for money. I gave it to him, so I could sleep. I was pregnant with my third baby and working second shift at a Waffle House; I was too tired to keep going back and forth with Keith.

Keith and Mommy continued getting high; this was a sad sight. *I oftentimes hated going home. If it weren't for my children, I wouldn't have gone back.* Keith lost his job. My stepfather and I were the only two working. Keith walked to Fulton Industrial to go to a Temp Service to earn enough money to give me a few dollars and buy some drugs. I was receiving a Social Security check on behalf of my father's disability when he was shot and paralyzed. Mommy had been receiving the check for years, but she finally turned it over to me. The check and working at Waffle House until I became too big to work, allowed us to stay in the apartment a little longer. But it didn't take long before the eviction notice was placed on the door.

We put the furniture in storage and moved into a rooming house in Atlanta. I hated having my children living in a rooming house. Mommy and my stepfather rented a large room with a separate bathroom, and Keith and I got a room with a kitchen. We shared the rooms and made the most out of it. I was eighteen with three beautiful children. Keith and I had a baby girl. My good friend Tonya who lived in the same apartment complex with her husband and children named her "Kendra." Kendra was a very pretty baby. She had big deer-like eyes, a cute puppy nose, and her skin complexion was light like her father's. I had to find a home for my children. I detested having them in a rooming house; it wasn't a place for kids.

> The eyes of the LORD are upon the righteous, and his ears are open unto their cry.
>
> —Psalm 34:15

There wasn't a day that went by while living in that rooming house that I didn't think about reaching out to Miles. Miles was one of my customers from Waffle House. He was an older, about forty, well kept, handsome gentleman who drove a truck for a living. Each time he came into town, he stopped by my job and offered to take me and my children on the road with him. He promised to buy us a house in any state I wanted to live and to take care of us. One day when he came into the Waffle House, he left his number and a note that said he was serious about his offer. I put the piece of paper in my pocket, and when I got home, I wrote the number on the wall in the corner of my closet and ripped the piece of paper into tiny pieces. I knew Keith would kill me if he saw it. Before we were evicted, I copied the phone number on a small piece of paper and placed it in my wallet. I was seriously contemplating calling Miles, but something inside just wouldn't let me do it.

We were living in the rooming house for about three months when I checked the mail and couldn't believe my eyes. The City of Marietta sent me an appointment date for a Section 8 Housing Voucher. I had forgotten we applied. I was told it would take a long time for my name to come up on the list, so I wasn't expecting anything this soon. I didn't know anything about Section 8 a year before this. My friend Tonya and I were riding around running some errands one day, and she suggested we go apply for Section 8. She heard about it or saw a flyer saying the City of Marietta was taking applications, so we went and applied. Two weeks after my appointment date, I received my voucher. I looked at the list of places and people in Marietta who accepted Section 8. I made appointments to check out the properties. One of the workers at the Section 8 office mentioned they had a new landlord on the list who recently joined the program. She explained the landlord just built two brand new apartment buildings. She suggested I look at them. I made my first appointment with this landlord. We met at the apartment building. The two buildings were all but complete, there were some odds and ends that needed to be taking care of, but the apartments were ready for occupancy.

When I saw the apartment buildings, I liked that they were nestled in the corner of a subdivision surrounded by nice houses. I had no desire to look at other properties. I couldn't wait to move to Marietta and leave the rooming house. I didn't have reliable transportation, a lot of furniture, or a job, but I was determined to move my children out of that rooming house. When I got my Social Security check, I purchased a very old car from a very old Black couple. I think the car was a 1969 Falcon, or something like that. The couple was honest and said the car would probably last only a few months and didn't need to be driven too far. This was good enough for me. We loaded that old car with our things and moved to Marietta.

...for your heavenly Father knows that ye have need of all these things.

—Matthew 6:32

Keith did help us move, and he stayed for the first couple of weeks. However, he couldn't live there because one of the Section 8 guidelines was no one could live with me and my children. This was a good thing for my situation. However, it wasn't a good guideline for all situations because it kept fathers away from their children, and probably caused more harm than good in the long run. By now, Mommy, both my sisters, and Keith were all addicted to crack. While my brother was running wild doing any and every illegal thing he wanted to do, which included selling crack. They all tried to live with us at one time or another, but I didn't want to take any chances on losing my voucher. I allowed them to stay for a few days, and then they had to leave.

I got our furniture, dishes, and other things out of storage. I rented a living room set and a washer and dryer. Someone in my family gave me an orange, yellow, and green striped dining room table with orange chairs. We didn't have much, but I was thankful and happy to finally have a stable place to live with my children, and I knew I didn't have to worry about Keith beating on me anymore! I went back to waitressing at Waffle House. My neighbor was very helpful; she watched children for a lot of people. She was able to watch my children while I worked.

Keith rode the Greyhound bus to visit over the weekend, but those visits became few and far between. I knew it would be a matter of time before the visits completely stopped. Because of his drug addiction, I used to have to meet him on his job every Friday at noon when he got paid in order to get money from him before he blew it on drugs. One Friday, I got a ride down to his job off Boulevard, and his supervisor told me he never returned from his lunch break. From that day forward, he was out of our lives; he never came back to Marietta. The beatings were finally over.

My times are in thy hand: deliver me from the hand of mine enemies, and from them that persecute me.

—Psalm 31:15

Something in the Atmosphere

I continued working, providing for my three children, and holding on to a gut feeling of wanting something better for myself and my children. Lindsay and Kenneth were now in school. One day I called Chattahoochee Technical School and inquired about getting my GED. I was told the process and given the next testing date. The clerk said I could sign-up to take prep classes. I didn't feel I needed them. On the day of the next test date, I walked to Chattahoochee Technical and took the exam for my GED. I passed the exam—this was a proud moment for me.

I can do all things through Christ which strengthens me.

—Philippians 4:13

Things were beginning to brighten. My children were okay, I had my GED, I was working double shifts to provide for my children, and I started liking a cook at the Waffle House named Terry. Once I knew Keith was gone for good, I started talking to him, and we eventually started a relationship. I really liked Terry. *I think I liked him because there wasn't any physical abuse, and I wasn't used to a man not abusing me.* Terry didn't seem to like me as much as I liked him. I knew he didn't think I was pretty enough to be his girlfriend; he just admired my body. I was very insecure about my looks and having three babies. *This made me feel as though my options were limited, so I demanded nothing and expected little.*

It didn't take long for me to see how little Terry really thought of or respected me. I'll never forget the day my friend Tonya came to the Waffle House to give me a ride home. Terry flirted with her knowing she was my friend and a married woman. Tonya knew I liked Terry, but I don't think she knew how much. She nicely blew off his advances while innocently smiling. My feelings were hurt, and I was embarrassed standing in the Waffle House watching Terry disregard me. The other workers knew he and I were messing around, and they witnessed the disrespect. I never said a word to either of them about how they hurt my feelings. Tonya was very pretty and gullible. I saw why Terry was attracted to her, and I knew he would eventually get to her. Terry continued to pursue Tonya. He finally got her attention, and they met up a couple of times.

Tonya was going through a rough patch with her husband; there was a rumor she had started smoking joints laced with crack cocaine. I never witnessed any of this. Her husband wanted to move his family back to Kentucky, but Tonya didn't want to leave Georgia. I remember telling Terry about the drug rumors, and his response was, "I don't care; I'll help her!" By this time, my one-sided relationship with Terry was over, and my friendship with Tonya became distant. I didn't see her getting high, but she started hanging with my sister Sabrina, and I knew Sabrina and her friends were doing drugs. I was glad when Tonya's husband moved them back to Kentucky. It was just a matter of time before Tonya lost control. She never did get a chance to use her Section 8 voucher.

Now that Tonya was gone, Terry and I were back at our one-sided relationship, mostly sexual partners. Our one-sided relationship went on like this for a few years. There was a time or two when Terry and I sincerely tried to make it work, but we had too many issues. He didn't want me, but he didn't want anyone else to have me. During our process of trying to make it work, I became pregnant. I told Terry I didn't want any more children. I was adamant about not having four children at the age of twenty-one. Terry and I agreed that an abortion would be best. I worked even more double shifts and saved the money to get the abortion.

For out of the heart proceed evil thoughts, murders...

—Matthew 15:19

The day before the scheduled abortion, Terry stole the

abortion money. I was furious. I went next door to my neighbor's house and called his home. My phone was disconnected because I needed all my money for the abortion. Terry's father answered the phone. I told his father what happened, and to my surprise, his father ministered to me about abortion being a sin and God not being pleased with it. He asked me to please not kill the baby. He promised he would do everything he could to help me. He also told me Terry spoke with him about the abortion and told him he took the money to keep me from aborting his child. I promised his father I wouldn't abort the baby. I hung up the phone and ran home, where I cried. I couldn't understand why Terry never told me he wanted me to keep the baby.

I kept my word and did not go through with the abortion. Terry was rarely around during my pregnancy; however, his father kept his word and helped me every step of the way. He was not only there for his grandson, but he was also there for my other children. The night my water broke, I drove myself to the hospital from Marietta to Atlanta. I called Terry's father. He was there as soon as I brought my cute, curly-haired baby boy into the world. He was there before Terry. Terry didn't come until the next day. He named our son Allen. I thank God for stopping the abortion, and I thank God for Allen's grandfather, who was a Godsend in more ways than one.

A man's heart devises his way: but the LORD directs his steps.

—Proverbs 16:9

My relationship with Terry continued off and on for a few more years. During this crazy time, I purchased my first car from a dealership. It was a Ford Festiva. We left the apartment and moved into a house in Marietta. It wasn't the best house, but I was excited because it had a back yard. My new neighbor Brenda was a nice person. We got along fine as neighbors. She had four children who were a little older than my children. The house never felt like a home;

it needed a lot of repairs, but the landlords were cheap and always tried to take short cuts with repairs. We lived there for almost two years before I found us a new home in Smyrna.

We moved into a nice little house on Birch Street in Smyrna for about a year before things started getting hectic. Mommy found out she was HIV positive and had colon cancer; she moved in with us for a little while. As soon as she left, my sister Teresa and her newborn baby moved in with us. Teresa had the baby while she was quarantined in Rome, Georgia for tuberculosis; no one knew she was pregnant. Teresa constantly left her baby with me for days. I threatened to call Child Protective Services, hoping she would come to get her baby, but it didn't work. One day a nurse from The Department of Health came to check in with my sister, her baby, and us. We all had to take a tuberculosis test, and The Department of Health was always sending someone to the house to check on us.

As usual, my sister wasn't there. The nurse was concerned. She said she had to report this information to the social worker, and true to her word, the nurse sent a social worker out to the house within a few days of her visit. The social worker looked around the house and asked me a lot of questions about my lifestyle and my children. She then began asking questions about Teresa and the baby. She asked, "Is Teresa back on drugs? Does she come see the baby? Do you think she has abandoned the baby? Is this a lot on you?" The social worker wrote notes while questioning me. When she was finished, she looked at me and said she had to take the baby with her. I didn't question or fight it. I thought this was what was needed for my sister to come to her senses.

Later that day, I started feeling horrible about my beautiful niece being taken. I felt as though it was my fault for honestly answering the social worker's questions. I rode around Marietta trying to find my sister; I needed to tell her what happened. When I did find my sister, her attitude was very nonchalant. I told her the social worker said they would mail a date and time for a Hearing, and we had to show up in order to get back the baby. I also told her that the social worker said she should reach out to her before the hearing to help her get back her baby.

...Let not your heart be troubled, neither let it be afraid.

—John 14:27

The letter with the date and time of the hearing arrived; I made sure my sister knew the date and time. The day of the hearing, I arrived early. I looked around to see if my sister had beat me there; I didn't see her. Each time the door opened, I jerked around hoping it was her. I wanted her to get her baby. I was prepared to help her and the baby, but deep in my heart, I knew my sister wouldn't show. She had already walked away and left her first two children with their father. After about thirty minutes of waiting for Teresa to show up, it was time for the hearing to start. Someone came to the lobby and called our names. My sister never came to fight for her baby. The last I heard, my niece was put up for adoption, and she was adopted by a wonderful couple who was unable to conceive. *I have always carried a sense of guilt and heaviness; I felt like I should have fought to get my niece.*

During our time in the house on Birch St., I believe I was trying to figure out exactly who I wanted to be as a person and woman. My life had no direction or guidance. Allen's grandfather continued to minister to me about giving my life to Christ; as a matter of fact, he ministered to my mother and my siblings. I listened to his words, but I didn't know what to do with the words I heard. But God knew what to do with them. He allowed his words to begin to take root in my heart, and I wasn't even aware that this was happening. While this was happening, I continued to smoke marijuana and I even went downtown and got a license to dance in a strip club. I tried dancing for two days and realized it wasn't who I was, nor was it what I wanted to do with my life. I remember the aura of the club feeling dark and dirty. I knew this would lead to a dead end. When I initially went and got the dancing license, I told myself it would be a way of earning some income, but I knew in my heart I was doing it to make Terry jealous, and it worked!

After the strip club debacle, I continued looking for a job. I finally ended up with a job managing a tire shop. I didn't know anything about managing a tire shop. The owner saw me standing at the bus stop near his business, and he spoke. We started a conversation, and I told him I was looking for a job. He offered me a job. I told him I didn't know anything about tires. He told me to just show up. I showed up the next day, and he taught me everything I needed to know. He taught me how to sell tires, paint used tires, balance tires, the different sizes of tires, and how long it took to put on and take off tires. I opened and closed the shop, I sold tires, kept the shop clean, ran errands, and paid the workers. I worked for him for about three years. The owner and I became very good friends. I was there during his first divorce, second marriage, death of his brother and sister, and the birth of his first child. "

…I have been with you at all seasons.

—Acts 20:18

My first three children were in elementary school; they were growing up, and we needed more space. I found a nice three-story townhouse. The owner was a nice old lady. The townhouse was well kept and had more than enough space, so we moved into our second home in Smyrna.

We moved next door to a family full of adults. It was a mother who lived with her adult children and a couple of grandchildren. One of the adults was my age. She and I started hanging out. We went to cookouts and smoked weed. She hung out quite often. She had only one child, and her family helped her take care of her child. I didn't have anyone to help me watch my children, and now, I had Sabrina's baby. He was born in prison, and she asked me to please take him until she was released in six months; I did. A few months after I got my nephew, Mommy had to move back in with us; she had AIDS. Mommy had nowhere to go, and the man she was living with was murdered. I had to take her in. I didn't want that responsibility, but I did what I had to do. There were a couple of times when I got the chance to hang out with my neighbor. This happened when Sabrina's friend came to get the baby for a night or two. This gave me a little freedom. I made sure my kids were settled for the evening and Mommy was okay and resting before I would go hang out with my neighbor. My friend's mother offered to look in on the kids and Mommy. She said I needed a break.

Be still and know that I am God...

—Psalm 46:10

I was grateful for the hospice nurses who came by a few times a week to help take care of Mommy. Watching my mother gradually shrivel up and die was very hard on me and the kids. At times, some of my family members dropped by for brief visits. They brought food, money, pampers, and other things for Mommy, but none of them offered to sit with her long enough to give me a break. They had no idea what it was like, and I never bothered to tell them or complain. Sabrina and Carey were incarcerated, and Teresa was in the streets getting high. They too, were not there to help me see about Mommy.

The prison system did allow my brother Carey to be escorted to the church to view Mommy's body on the day of the funeral before anyone else arrived at the church. We knew he had visited because he signed the guest book.

The morning I went in Mommy's room to check on her and saw that she had passed away was a sad day, but yet a relief. I never slowed down to mourn. I remember sort of breezing through my mother's funeral. I was hurt and angry. I said out loud around my family, "Why did it have to be my mother?" I can still hear my aunt yell my name "Christie!". I knew, in her way, she was scolding me for wishing it was someone else. I didn't care. While riding in the creepy family car, we approached Causey Chapel Church. I blurted out just before we got to the church, "That's where Mommy and my daddy conceived me, behind that church." I don't know why I felt a need to say that, but I did. If looks could kill, my grandmother gave me the meanest look ever. I knew she wanted to slap me in the middle of next week. But what could she do, we were on our way to bury her daughter, my mother? I thought about the conversation Mommy and my grandmother had before Mommy passed away. My mother was admitted into the hospital for complications from AIDS, and I was in the room visiting when my grandmother walked in. They started talking, and I heard my mother say, "I never thought you loved me." My grandmother responded, "How could I not love you? You were the first child I ever loved." I couldn't help but think, *That's how I feel about you. Do you love me Mommy?*

We finally arrived at the church. It was crowded. Mommy knew a lot of people. My grandmother put Mommy away nicely; Mommy had written her final wishes in 1990. *This may have been when she first found out she was HIV positive.* She gave the letter to my aunt Stephanie who gave it to me. *I still have the letter of her final wishes.* My grandmother didn't follow Mommy's wishes verbatim. Mommy was buried under the oak tree, she got the spray she wanted, and she was buried in her favorite colors of lavender and pink. The only thing grandma didn't do was have the songs Mommy requested. After the internment and repass, I went home, changed my clothes, and spent time consoling my kids and nephew. I didn't seem to feel anything.

A few days after Mommy's funeral, I started hanging out with my friend a little too much. Early one morning, I got home and realized I had been away from my children and home for quite a few hours. This frightened me. I walked upstairs to lie down, but when my head hit the pillar, I could feel my heart loudly pounding. It felt like it was going to jump out of my chest. I thought I was about to die. I sat up, thinking this would help relax me. While sitting there, I thought about what I had been doing, and how I almost went to jail. This frightened me even more, and my heart pounded even harder.

An hour before I got home, my neighbor and I were in the apartment complex next door to where we lived; there were two other people in the car with us. I don't know why we were there, but I know we were getting high by smoking lace joints. It was about four o'clock in the morning, and we were heading out of the apartment complex toward the gate when we saw flashing lights. I remember someone was in the backseat, and my neighbor was in the front passenger seat. The smell of marijuana mixed with cocaine was strong. I knew we were on our way to jail; at least I would be going to jail because it was my car. Once we got to the gate, the officers flashed their flashlights in the car and said they were looking for someone. I believe they said there had been a robbery in the complex. They told us to go on through the gate.

And the LORD shall help them, and deliver them...

—Psalm 37:40

I couldn't drive home fast enough. I didn't drop anyone off at his or her house. I drove directly to my house, and everyone dispersed in my driveway. Now I'm sitting on the edge of my bed afraid I'm about to die because my heart is pounding like hail beating on a roof. I got up and went into the girl's room and awoke Lindsay. I told Lindsay I was going to the hospital because my heart was pounding. I didn't tell her all the details. I also called my pastor, Allen's grandfather, and told him I was going to the hospital. I told him what I had done. I hadn't officially joined his church, but we were beginning to attend regularly.

I walked into Smyrna Hospital's Emergency Room. When they took me back, and asked me what was wrong, I told them my heart was beating too fast. They examined me and asked if anything had happened to cause my rapid heartbeat. I told them I believe it was because I had smoked marijuana laced with cocaine. About fifteen minutes later, someone came into the room and asked me if I would like to go to a place for a couple of days in order to get some rest and help. They never referred to the place as a rehab facility, and I never thought about it being a rehab facility. I just knew the thought of getting some rest and being away from everybody and everything for a day or two sounded great. I told them I had kids and needed to make some arrangements. They didn't judge me or give me that "sure" look; they simply handed me the information and told me the people would be expecting me.

The LORD our God spoke unto us in Horeb, saying, Ye have dwelt long enough in this mount

—Deuteronomy 1:6

I found myself checking into what seemed to be a very peaceful place. I still didn't exactly know what type of establishment the place was. The people were friendly and welcoming. Brenda's friend Nate drove me there; it was a silent rainy drive. I wasn't sure of the location, but I knew it was near Kennesaw. I started to miss my children, but I was thankful my friend Brenda had agreed to keep Lindsay, Kenneth, and Kendra. She is a good person, and I trusted her with them. I knew Allen was in good hands with his grandfather.

It rained the entire weekend; I slept a lot. When I awoke, I ate, talked with a counselor, and slept some more. I didn't recall the conversations, but I do remember the conversations were relaxing. I knew I was done with that brief stint of drug use in my life. When Sunday came, they gave me information for attending drug meetings. I didn't need it. Somehow, I knew I was done with that part of my life, but I took the information anyway and attended a few meetings. By the grace of God, it took me one weekend away from my children to realize I was on the path of destruction, and I wasn't having that. I went home, got my children, and from that Sunday forward, with God's help, I was determined to change the trajectory of our lives.

For I know the thoughts that I think toward you, saith the LORD, thoughts of peace, and not of evil, to give you an expected end.

—Jeremiah 29:11

Soon after my hospital incident, I started working at King Springs Assisted Living. The job was in walking distance from the house. I worked in the dining room serving the residents. The job was easy, and I was a good employee. One day while walking home from work, I saw a flyer for a "Cobb County School Bus Driver". The flyer listed date and time for applicants to apply. My next day at work, I told my supervisor, Linda Devereaux, I needed to take off to go apply for the bus driver job. *I don't know why I told her; I think I thought she would be happy for me.* She looked at me with a very stern look and said, "If you take off to go apply for that job, you can never work here again!" I was stunned.

The enemy shall not exact upon him; nor the son of wickedness afflict him.

—Psalm 89:22

Although I was stunned by her reaction, Ms. Devereaux's words didn't stop me. I took off and went and applied for the bus driver position. I never worked at King Springs Assisted Living again! I got the job with Cobb County Schools. The job didn't come easy. I applied and waited and waited to hear back from Cobb County Schools. One day a woman called and said, "Ms. Waldon, we want to hire you, but there's something coming back on your background check." I was shocked. I had no idea what it could be. The woman told me to go to the courthouse in Marietta to check on it and let her know once everything was straightened out. I went the very next day.

When I got to the courthouse to see the clerk, they told me there was a closed case with my name. My neighbor I hung out with sold her cousin's old abandoned car without his permission, unbeknownst to me. Her cousin filed a police report and included my name. One day the police stopped me while I was driving and said there was a warrant for my arrest for theft. They took me to jail. I called my grandparents, and they came and bailed me out. I was furious because I had nothing to do with her selling his abandoned car. I knew in my heart he included my name because I was friends with his cousin, and he used to try to get me to go out with him, and I never would go. I never received a court date to defend myself, so this came as a big surprise.

The Court Clerk told me the charges had been dropped because the cousin never followed up. She said I had to speak with the District Attorney. Once I walked into his office, he began questioning me about what happened, and I told him. He told me it would be removed from my record, but he stressed only because he couldn't get the guy to follow through. I believe he really wanted to charge me with something, but they had to remove it from my record. I asked them for a letter stating this case been dropped, and I had not been charged with anything. They gave me a letter, and I took it to Cobb County Schools.

What shall we then say to these things? If God be for us, who can be against us?

—Romans 8:31

Once I gave Cobb County Schools the letter, they gave me a date for training. I did well with my training and started driving a school bus for the upcoming school year. I was proud of my job driving a school bus. I took my job seriously. I really enjoyed the students and the hours. I was afforded time to spend with my children when they were out of school for breaks, and I was able to go volunteer at their school. I became very involved in their education.

While volunteering at Allen's school, his teacher, Shawn Lyday, looked at me and said, "Ms. Waldon, you're good with kids; why don't you become a teacher?" A thought like that had never crossed my mind. No one had ever told me I was good at anything, and I only had a GED.

And he hath put a new song in my mouth, even praise unto our
God: many shall see it, and fear, and shall trust in the LORD.

—Psalm 40:3

Her words stuck with me, and I started looking into enrolling in
a University. I didn't know the first step to take. I mailed letters to
universities telling them I wanted to enroll. No one ever responded.
I guess they figured I didn't belong in a university if I didn't know
how to apply. One day I overheard a conversation about student
loan refunds. I asked more questions and found out there was money
available for me to go to school. Someone shared the process with me,
and I applied for grants and loans. I had to list on the application the
universities I wanted to attend. I listed Kennesaw State and Georgia
State Universities on my application. Kennesaw State accepted me
first, and I immediately began registering for classes.

It didn't take long before I looked up and was sitting on Kennesaw
State's campus in orientation. I remember the facilitator's stressing to
"non-traditional" students such as myself, *I didn't know there was a
name for a student such as myself,* the importance of always having a
"Plan B." They said to view the "Plan B" like an inclement weather
plan; it's good to have one while hoping to never need it. I took this
and other advice they provided to heart. *This advice came in handy
several times.* I was also considered a "PCP," which stood for Parking
Lot-Classroom-Parking Lot student, which meant I was only there
for business.

Though thy beginning was small, yet thy latter end should greatly
increase.

—Job 8:7

Being on a college campus was intimidating and tough in the
beginning, but I soon found out I didn't have time to be intimidated,
I had to put my energy into studying and applying myself. Due to

having been out of school for a while, I had to start off with remedial math and English courses. I remember feeling a little embarrassed about this, but I soon realized I wasn't alone. Several students had to take remedial classes. One of the two Black professors I had throughout my entire college career taught the remedial English class, and the other taught history.

The English Professor had dreadlocks. Her presence gave me a sense of belonging. She was a good instructor. I remember her reassuring me that my not being able to type fast wouldn't have a bearing on my passing the course. I also remember she and I had a few personal conversations. I'll always remember her sharing with me that although she was remarried, her first husband was her true love but he passed away. The other professor was a handsome Black male. He was also a great instructor. We had good rich conversations in his classes about history. I was stunned to find out his family did not descend from slavery. I assumed all black people in the United States descended from slavery.

My bus driving work schedule aligned perfectly with my class schedule; this was a blessing from God. I dropped off my load of students at Campbell Middle School and got in my minivan and headed up interstate seventy-five to get to class. It worked out where my routes were the first to unload at the school in the morning. I was also able to make it back with a little time to spare before picking up my afternoon load. My routes were in the community where we lived. My children often rode the bus with me. We got home, ate, and studied together. There were times when my children were in bed, and I would sit struggling into the early morning hours because my studies hit me like a tsunami; I cried and pressed my way many nights.

...but David encouraged himself in the LORD his God.

—1 Samuel 30:6

When I didn't have classes, I worked in the school cafeteria serving lunch, or worked in schools as a substitute teacher. At least twice a week, one of my coworkers would see me sitting on my school bus reading and or studying while waiting for my load of students to be dismissed and ask, "Are you still in school?". I knew they were expecting me to quit, but they didn't know how determined I was to bring a change of season into my life and the lives of my children. Nothing was going to stop me. I knew this is what I was meant to do, and regardless of the challenges, I was determined to see it through.

The vicissitudes of life continued to come; they didn't care that I was in school trying to better myself and make a better life for my children. They did their job and came and went like the winter season. While I was going through school, 9/11 happened, my oldest son Kenneth decided he wanted to join the military as a show of his patriotism, and my youngest son Allen started acting out in school. I was sitting in class when all the buzz started. I had no clue about what was happening. They canceled classes for the day. I left campus and continued with my plans. I went to *Bank of America* on the square in Marietta. While standing in line, the magnitude of what had just happened hit me. People were discussing how terrorists had flown planes into the Twin Towers. They were saying America was under siege. People were at the bank trying to get their money. I didn't have much to get and wasn't sure if that was what I should do. I completed my transaction and left. By the time I got home that evening, replays of the planes flying into the buildings were on every news station. I couldn't believe my eyes when I saw the airplanes fly into the towers and explode. This day was infamously dubbed 9/11.

Kenneth came home from school about a week after 9/11 and said he wanted to join the Army. He said he had already spoken with a recruiter, and this was his patriotic duty. He gave me the card and paperwork the recruiter had given him. He said the recruiter wanted to come by and talk with me. I told Kenneth I didn't think this was a good idea. I told him it would be much different from the ROTC. He asked me to please meet and listen to the recruiters. I agreed and called them to set up a date to meet and talk. The recruiters came to the house; it was two of them. They tried to convince me that this was a great move for Kenneth. I knew Kenneth was highly intelligent and had other options. I also knew the military wouldn't work for Kenneth because he had such a free kind spirit about himself, and this decision was one of impulse and excitement. I tried with everything in me to convince him not to enlist, but he didn't listen.

Once I realized he had committed and was due to report to Basic Training immediately after his graduation, there was nothing I could do. I left it in God's hands. Kenneth's High School Graduation ceremony in 2002, was an emotional bitter-sweet time for me. I was proud of my son for graduating high school and equally proud of him for wanting to serve his country, but I didn't want him to leave. I knew deep down inside this wasn't the route for him. It turns out, I was right.

Now the Lord of peace himself give you peace always by all means. The Lord be with you all...

—2 Thessalonians 3:16

Something was going on with Allen. At least once a week, I was getting a call from one of his teachers. They said Allen's behavior had become hostile; he wasn't doing his work or listening to his teachers. I had a talk with his father. He and I agreed that it might be best if Allen lived with him for a minute. I told Allen if his behavior continued down this path, I would send him to live with his father. Two weeks after this conversation, we got a call from school saying Allen had been suspended for throwing a chair at his teacher. I was flabbergasted! During his suspension, he moved in with his father. This arrangement lasted for only two months. Each time I called to check on my child, his father wouldn't be there, and my child was always eating *Wendy's* for dinner. My son wanted to come home, and I knew he needed to come home. Once he came home, his behavior changed. We later found out what was bothering Allen. It was shocking.

Even during the winter months, the sun still comes up. Not everything that happened during this time was bad. Lindsay attended her Senior prom; she was gorgeous. She wore a long fitted blue gown that glittered. She wore a very short haircut and a little make-up. Her date wore a white tuxedo. They were a very handsome couple. Lindsay also graduated high school. It was one of the proudest moments of my life, seeing my daughter walk across that stage and get her high school diploma. I cried tears of joy. I couldn't believe my first-born child had just done what I wasn't able to do. I spared no expense in making her graduation party a huge affair. I invited our family members; a lot of them came and supported her during this milestone moment. It was a beautiful day. Lindsay received several gifts, accolades, and well wishes. One of my happiest moments of the party was the look on her face when she saw her cake. I had Publix put a picture of her beautiful face on the cake.

Lindsay was a great child and an even better young woman. We had some growing pains, but nothing too major. Most of the growing pains stemmed from my wanting her to forever remain "my" little girl. She had a boyfriend and was working. She worked herself up to a manager at Chick-Fil-A. Lindsay knew she would go to college, but she wasn't sure of a major. She used to want to be a journalist. I remember taking her to WSB Television Studio, where she met and spent time with Karen Minton. They allowed her to sit at the anchor desk and get a feel for what it was like. Somewhere along the way, Lindsay changed her mind about that. I didn't pressure Lindsay about college. I knew she would get around to it, and she did.

In those days they shall say no more, The fathers have eaten a sour grape, and the children's teeth are set on edge.

—Jeremiah 31:29

A Palm Tree in the Storm

Due to 9/11, Kenneth committed to joining the Army and Allen's charade; one would think the seasons were due to change. March 12, 2002 said otherwise. I was at home in the basement on the computer doing my homework. The computer kept kicking me offline. Back then, it was the very slow DSL connected to the phone lines. After about an hour of rebooting, I finally gave up and decided I would try later. As soon as I got off the computer, the phone was ringing. I picked it up and said, "hello." It was a nurse from the hospital on the other end of the phone. She told me I needed to come to the hospital because my sister was very sick. I told her I would be there as soon as I could. I didn't think much about it; I just thought Sabrina must have had a very bad sickle cell crisis while in jail, and they needed me to come to the hospital to fill out or sign some paperwork. Before I left to go to the hospital, I called my pastor and asked him to pray for my sister. He asked me which hospital they had taken her to and said he would be praying.

When the kids and I got to the hospital, I saw my aunt Stephanie standing outside; she was smoking a cigarette and talking with someone. I still didn't think anything about seeing her there. The kids and I went up to my sister's floor. Once we got there, I saw my pastor sitting in the waiting area. I walked over and thanked him for being there, and I remembered thinking to myself, he could have prayed for Sabrina from home. I went to the nurses' station and asked to see my sister. The nurse told me I had to wait. I waited for what seemed hours, but it was only about fifteen minutes. I became impatient waiting for them to let me go see her; I was starting to get nervous and anxious. I got up and stormed through the double doors looking for my sister; it didn't take long for me to find her. There she lay dead in the first room to my left. I stood frozen, staring at my sister's lifeless body. She had one tear lodged in the corner of her eye. That tear spoke volumes; death didn't wait for her to drop that last tear from her eye where I could see many had already fallen and dried.

My sister was dead! I couldn't move; I just looked in her face waiting to hear her say, as she always did, "Don't worry, Chris, I'm alright." Those words never came. I stood there with a thousand thoughts running through my mind. I wondered about her last words and thoughts. I wanted to know if she knew I was on the way. I wanted to know if she were afraid. I wondered if she had time to repent, and most importantly, I wanted to know "Why?" I was frozen in time when I finally felt someone's arms around me. I looked up, and it was the security guard. She told me she prayed with Sabrina before she passed away. I gathered all the strength I could and walked out to the waiting area. I had to tell the children. Lindsay knew because she had walked back there with me.

The LORD God is my strength and he will make my feet like hinds' feet...

—Habbakah 3:19

We were truly hurt; the kids and I sat at the hospital in the waiting area for a long time. My nephew's daddy and his wife brought him to the hospital. He wanted to stay with us, so they left him at the hospital with us. I guess my nephew needed to be close to his mother's immediate family. Everyone except for my pastor left us there at the hospital. I knew I had to quickly pull myself together because I had to claim my sister's body and prepare to make funeral arrangements. I didn't know what to do or where to start. My pastor asked me if I had any money. I told him I had saved fifteen-hundred dollars. He called *Andrews Mortuary*. It didn't take the mortician a long time to come get my sister's body.

We finally left the hospital and went home. The kids and I stayed awake almost all night. We talked about the last time we saw Sabrina alive. We also talked about the good memories before the drug use.

70

About six months before her passing, Lindsay and I begged Sabrina to leave the drugs and streets alone. I told her she could continue to stay with us. She had just had part of one of her lungs removed; the doctor said her lungs were full of black gunk and pneumonia. Sabrina stayed in the hospital for a week, and then she came to the house to stay with us for a few more days. She stayed long enough to build up her strength, and she headed back to the streets. We desperately tried to help her break her crack addiction. When she left that day, I saw her one more time before she died, and we weren't on the best of terms that last time.

After healing from her surgery, Sabrina left Smyrna and went back to doing what she did. A month after she left our house, she called me and said she was going to stop by because there was something, she needed to tell me. She quickly said, "It's good." We hung up and I thought about the good news she could possibly have. My thoughts of good news were of her going into a drug rehabilitation center. When Sabrina got to the house, she was with a much older White man; he looked to be in his late sixties. I waited to hear what she had to say. Sabrina introduced the man and said she was no longer living in the hotel on Fulton Industrial; she was now living with her new man, and they were planning to get married. The old man showed me the engagement ring he had purchased for my sister; it was a very nice ring. I still have the ring in my possession; when Sabrina passed away, the old man gave it to me. He said it belonged to Sabrina, and he wanted me to have it. I was surprised to hear this. I thought to myself...*Has my sister told this man she is HIV positive and more than likely now has AIDS?*

When I got a chance to be alone with Sabrina, I asked her if she had told "her" man about her HIV. Sabrina looked at me while biting her lip, *which is something she always did when she was high,* and said, "No, Chris; I'm gonna tell him!" With that, she and her old sugar daddy headed out the door. This was the very last time I saw my sister alive. A few weeks later, I received a three-way call from

71

the jail; it was Sabrina. She told me she would probably have to do a few months. She wanted me to keep in touch with the old man and help him put money on her books. She reiterated they were still going to get married once she was released. I asked Sabrina if she had finally told him about her situation. She told me it wasn't any of my business. I told her what she was doing was wrong. That was our last conversation. *In retrospect, Sabrina was right, it wasn't my business; they were two adults.* It wasn't hard to look at Sabrina and tell something was wrong. She was a skeleton in a frame, and unlike Mommy's face, her face was covered with black spots and lesions. She couldn't take two steps without gasping for breath. Despite all of that, it was still easy to see that Sabrina was once very pretty.

The next day, our family and friends came by to pay their respects. We cried, reminisced, and ate. After that evening, I didn't have any more time to reminisce or mourn my sister's death. I had to get to work planning her funeral, and I had to try and console her boys as well as my children. I thank God Sabrina's oldest son Jeremiah and my children were all teenagers. Allen was twelve and Deitric was eight. We all loved Sabrina. I especially loved Sabrina, and she loved me. Outside of my children, I felt like she was the only person in the world who genuinely loved me. She never called me ugly or made me feel that I was ugly. Sabrina was a good big sister to me, and an awesome aunt to her nieces and nephews; she was especially close with Lindsay. Sabrina loved her boys, but her crack addiction was stronger than her love for herself or anyone, including her boys. March 16, 2002, my sister was laid to rest.

...for he hath said, I will never leave thee, nor forsake thee.

—Hebrews 13:5

Retelling this part of my story has been the hardest thus far. At times, I cried like a baby. It felt like I had just burst through those double doors looking for my sister. I wasn't sure I would be able to get through this part of the story...eighteen years later!

During my last year of college, my nephew Jeremiah came to live with us. His father put him out of the house on his eighteenth birthday. He didn't put him out because he displayed "bad" behavior. Jeremiah was a good child considering all he had gone through. His father married a mean woman who did not like my nephew. I'll never forget my nephew calling and asking me to come get him the evening of his mother's funeral. His wicked stepmother looked at him and said, "If you don't want to go with us, we can take you back and leave you on your mother's grave!" *She has since apologized for her words and actions.* I had no problem bringing my nephew into my home. He didn't stay with us more than six months. He continued working hard and saving his money and eventually got his own apartment.

This was also the year I finally and completely gave my life to Christ, not to say everything was perfect, but I matured enough to come in from the rain. I started tuning into the voice of Holy Spirit. I spent more time in prayer and studying the word. I slowly started pulling away from sin. I made sure we remained faithful to the Lord and going to church. I started a bible study in my home for children in the community. My pastor, who was now my Bishop, was a very good man. He truly gave his all to practice the lifestyle he preached, and he demonstrated what true love really is. He taught me the importance of showing people you love them and not just saying it with your mouth.

This is my commandment, That ye love one another, as I have loved you.

—John 15:12

He also drilled the importance of keeping one's word.

...but he honors them that fear the LORD. He that swears to his own hurt and change not.

—Psalm 15:4

73

Graduation day for me finally arrived. This day was so many things wrapped in one. It was the prom I never attended, the high school graduation I never had and the breaking of a cycle of generational curses. I couldn't believe I was standing here in Kennesaw State's University auditorium in my cap and gown about to walk across the stage to get my college diploma in education! My family was there to witness this graduation. It warmed my heart to look out and see my children and grandparents in the audience. They were all very proud of me. I remember wishing Mommy, Sabrina, Teresa, and my brother Carey were there to see me graduate. I knew they too would have been very proud. I changed my sad frame of thinking and went home and celebrated. I had a bottle of champagne with my name written on the bottle. *Before you start gasping, I was in line with the word.*

> The aged women, likewise, that they be in behavior as becometh holiness, not false accusers, not given to much wine, teachers of good things...
>
> —Titus 2:3

After my brief graduation celebration, I had to hit the ground running. I had to prepare to take custody of my youngest nephew, Deitric. He was now living with my grandparents, and some of my relatives didn't like this, so my grandparents asked me if I would take him. Before moving in with my grandparents, my nephew lived with my sister's aunt on her father's side. When she got out of prison, she came and got her baby, who was then six months old. Soon after she got him from me, she went back to using drugs and one day left my nephew in a hotel room where the housekeeper found him wet, hungry, and crying. The housekeeper called the police.

My sister was located and arrested for child abandonment. Sabrina sobered up long enough to ask her aunt to get custody of her son. Her aunt did. We visited Deitric at her house, and she often took him to visit my grandparents. Deitric asked to live with my grandparents, and they agreed which is how he ended up with my grandparents, thus ultimately in my care. I asked them to give me time to finish school. They agreed, and I remained involved in Deitric's home and school life until I graduated. The week I graduated from college; my grandparents brought my nephew to my house to live with us. I took this in stride and continued with life. I had to prepare to start my job as a teacher; it was coming in a month.

Afterword

With all the fog in my life, my visibility was very low. I couldn't see what was ahead, but God knew what was ahead because he was in the details consistently guiding and steering my path from the moment I was conceived and brought into this world, March 23, 1969, at 1:19 AM. God made the crooked paths straight when I was and was not aware of his presence in my life. I hope this part of my life encourages you to know and believe that God is in the details, whether you know it or not, and Philippians 4:13 is true! "I can do all things through Christ which strengtheneth me" (KJV). Be blessed and stay tuned because the storms have not ceased being part of my life, but neither has God.

CPSIA information can be obtained
at www.ICGtesting.com
Printed in the USA
LVHW010230150121
676361LV00013B/665